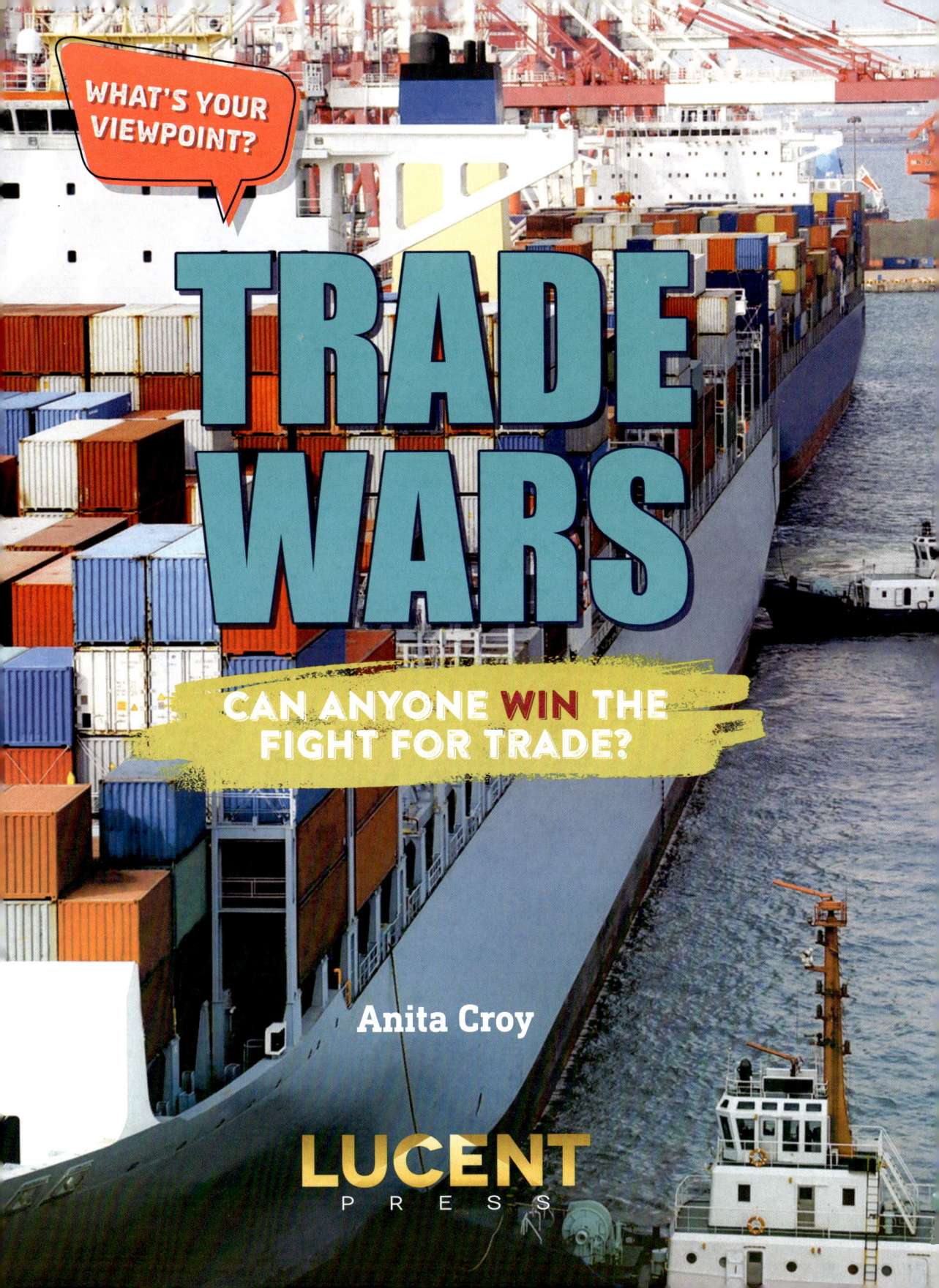

Published in 2020 by
Lucent Press, an Imprint of Greenhaven Publishing, LLC
353 3rd Avenue
Suite 255
New York, NY 10010

Copyright © 2020 Lucent Press, an Imprint of Greenhaven Publishing, LLC.

All rights reserved. No part of this book may be reproduced in any form without permission in writing from the publisher, except by a reviewer.

Produced for Lucent by Calcium
Editors: Sarah Eason and Tim Cooke
Designers: Paul Myerscough and Lynne Lennon
Picture researcher: Rachel Blount

Picture credits: Cover: Shutterstock: William Perugini (fg), Tcly (bg). Inside: Shutterstock: Arindambanerjee: p. 26; Barry Barnes: p. 17; ChameleonsEye: p. 30; CookieWei: p. 22; Creative Caliph: p. 40; DSBurnside: p. 31; Everett – Art: p. 8; Everett Historical: p. 10; John Gress Media Inc: p. 32; HelloRF Zcool: p. 12; Humphery: p. 7; Praphan Jampala: p. 34; Jenson: p. 21; Joraca: p. 27; Jstone: pp. 6, 43; Zhao Jian Kang: p. 18; A Katz: p. 36; Kite_rin: p. 39; Diane Kuhl: p. 28; Abdul Razak Latif: p. 37; Matt Ledwinka: p. 9; Lightspring: p. 24; Lukassek: p. 38; Alexandros Michailidis: p. 15; MNBB Studio: pp. 11, 42; NextNewMedia: p. 29; Phuong D. Nguyen: p. 13; William Potter: p. 41; Mark Reinstein: p. 25; Romsvetnik: p. 20; Solis Images: p. 16; Sundry Photography: p. 35; Symbiot: p. 14; Tcly: p. 1; Tishomir: p. 33; TonyV3112: p. 19; Lee Yiu Tung: p. 4; Haobo Wang: p. 23.

Cataloging-in-Publication Data

Names: Croy, Anita.
Title: Trade wars: Can Anyone Win the Fight for Trade? / Anita Croy.
Description: New York : Lucent Press, 2020. | Series: What's your viewpoint?
| Includes glossary and index.
Identifiers: ISBN 9781534565630 (pbk.) | ISBN 9781534565647 (library bound)
| ISBN 9781534565654 (ebook)
Subjects: LCSH: International trade--Juvenile literature. | Commercial policy--
Juvenile literature.
Classification: LCC HF1379.C79 2020 | DDC 382'.3--dc23

Printed in the United States of America

CPSIA compliance information: Batch #BS19KL: For further information contact Greenhaven Publishing LLC, New York, New York at 1-844-317-7404.

Please visit our website, www.greenhavenpublishing.com. For a free color catalog of all our high-quality books, call toll free 1-844-317-7404 or fax 1-844-317-7405.

Contents

WHAT'S THE DEBATE? 4

CHAPTER ONE
TRADE WARS 6

CHAPTER TWO
FREE TRADE 12

CHAPTER THREE
CHINA 18

CHAPTER FOUR
NORTH AMERICAN FREE TRADE AGREEMENT 24

CHAPTER FIVE
JOBS AND EMPLOYMENT 30

CHAPTER SIX
CHANGING TRADE 36

TRADE WARS: WHAT'S NEXT? 42

THE FUTURE: WHAT'S YOUR VIEWPOINT? 44

Glossary 46
For More Information 47
Index 48

TRADE WARS

What's the Debate?

A trade war is a situation in which countries try to damage each other's trade to improve their own trade. They usually do this by using tariffs, which are taxes or payments that have to be paid when goods from a particular country are imported, or brought into, another country. Countries might also limit imports from overseas by using quotas. A quota is a maximum amount of goods that can be imported. Some politicians believe measures such as tariffs and quotas help protect a country's economy and jobs. However, most economists, or experts who study trade, believe such measures are harmful. They believe the best form of trade for everyone is free trade, in which goods pass easily among countries with no barriers to stop them.

This book looks at the debates surrounding international trade. Read each chapter to find out about one debate. Then examine the ✔ and ✘ features at the end of the chapter, which explain both sides of the debate. Finally, review the "What's Your Viewpoint?" feature at the end of the chapter to make up your own mind about the debate. You can also find out what viewpoint people in leading positions hold by reading the "What's Their Viewpoint?" features. Let's start by taking a look at two arguments about free trade.

Oil tanks line the harbor at Hong Kong in China. China's economy has grown rapidly in recent decades.

WHAT'S THE DEBATE?

DEBATING FREE TRADE

FOR FREE TRADE

- Free trade makes the world economy grow. That helps everyone, including some of the world's poorest countries, whose individual economies also grow.

- Countries that trade together usually get along better, so free trade helps reduce the chance of conflict and tension.

- Today's economy is global. Countries that join together in free trade agreements should grow wealthier.

- Putting up barriers to trade could have widespread effects, leading to a decline in world trade and possibly the start of an economic depression.

AGAINST FREE TRADE

- Free trade only benefits rich countries. It allows them to take advantage of cheap labor and cheap materials in developing countries.

- Free trade costs jobs in developed economies, because jobs are moved to countries where labor costs less.

- All countries need to have their own industries that are key for national security, such as energy supply or steelmaking.

- Free trade allows developing countries to steal ideas and technology from the countries that paid to develop them.

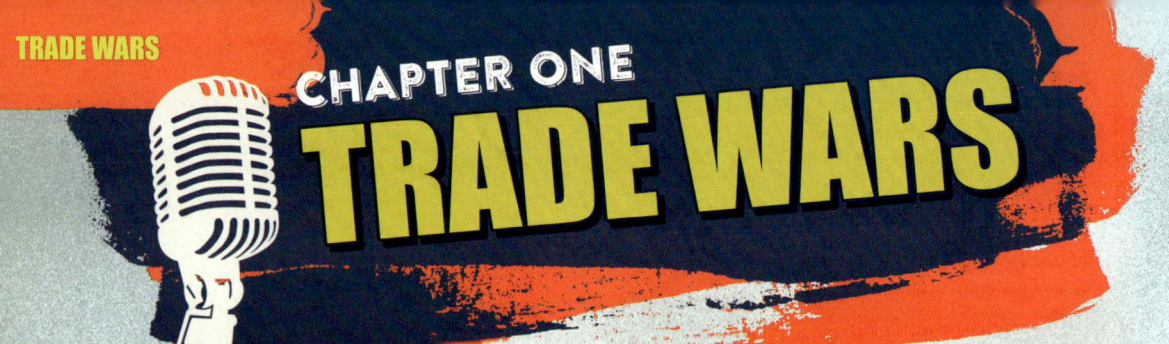

CHAPTER ONE
TRADE WARS

When Donald Trump became president of the United States in January 2017, he said he would change the way the country traded with the rest of the world. The president said that China was selling goods in America cheaper than they could be made in the United States. He also said the Chinese were stealing US ideas by illegally copying products and selling them cheaply.

The new president also complained about US membership in free trade agreements, which prevented members from limiting imports from other countries. In November 2017, Trump withdrew the United States from the Trans-Pacific Partnership (TPP). This was a free trade area of 12 countries around the Pacific Ocean, including Japan. Trump said that withdrawing would protect US workers by preventing many cheap imports.

Donald Trump claimed the United States got a bad deal in international trade.

The president also threatened to withdraw from the North American Free Trade Agreement (NAFTA), a deal signed by the United States, Mexico, and Canada in 1994. Trump argued that NAFTA allowed US firms to move jobs to Mexico and allowed Canada to sell cheap lumber in the United States. Trump said that unless the agreement was renegotiated, or discussed again, he would pull the United States out of NAFTA altogether.

TRADE WARS

A Businessman

One of the reasons Trump was elected president was because he had a reputation as a successful businessman. He had spent decades buying and selling real estate in New York City. He had taken his business experience onto TV, where he hosted a reality show called *The Apprentice*. The show tested the smarts of people who wanted a break in their business careers. Now that he was in the White House, Trump argued that he was very good at making deals. He claimed that other countries were laughing at the United States for allowing them to trade freely there. Trump promised Americans that he would improve the US economy by taking a tough line on international trade.

One of President Trump's main targets for criticism was the Chinese economy.

Causing Panic

Trump's attitude alarmed many economists, who believed that trade should not be controlled by laws or artificial limits. Instead, some argued that trade should be regulated only by the market, so businesses in different countries were free to make and sell anything wherever they could find buyers who would pay their prices. When Trump threatened to put tariffs on Chinese imports, economists warned this would increase the price US shoppers had to pay for goods. When he said US businesses should not make goods in Mexico, the Mexican government and many US businesspeople protested. However, many US workers were hopeful that Trump's plans would create more jobs in the United States.

TRADE WARS

A History of Trade

The best way to organize trade has been debated for centuries. In ancient times, most trade was local. People exchanged goods with their neighbors. As transportation improved, merchants began to move materials and goods over longer distances. Soon, trade routes ran across continents. By the second century BCE, silk from China was carried across Asia to Europe along the Silk Road, while glass, gold, and silver passed the other way. The trade of goods between countries flourished.

Merchants from the Netherlands grew rich, thanks to their fleet of trading ships.

In the 1400s and 1500s, European merchants sailed the world looking for goods such as spices from East Asia or furs from North America. Their governments backed them because the more trade a country had, the more taxes were paid and the more powerful the country became. Spain grew rich on American silver and Great Britain traded tea, while the wealth of the Netherlands relied on spices from East Asia.

Growth of Protectionism

As competition grew, countries began to protect their trade from foreign interference. They passed laws to prevent foreign merchants from trading in their countries, and tried to prevent them from learning about new technology. When the French developed a new kind of loom for weaving silk, for example, they banned weavers from taking the machines abroad, so they could not be copied. This approach is called protectionism.

WHAT'S THEIR VIEWPOINT?

A number of US presidents have been supporters of protectionism. They include George Washington, the first president, who said in 1789: "A free people ... should promote such manufactories [industries] as tend to render [make] them independent of others for essential, particularly military, supplies." Another supporter of protectionism was Abraham Lincoln in the 1860s. Lincoln talked about the damage free trade did to the United States: "I do not know much ... but I know this ... when we buy manufactured goods abroad, we get the goods and the foreigner gets the money. When we buy the manufactured goods at home, we get both the goods and the money."

Protectionism is based on the idea that trade should make money for a specific country. The more goods a country exports, or sells abroad, the more money it earns. The more a country buys foreign goods, the more money goes abroad. The country grows poorer, and workers lose their jobs. Governments therefore set out to protect their economies with regulations.

A New Idea

In the mid-1700s, a new idea emerged. It suggested that all countries would grow wealthier if they traded freely. Each nation should specialize. If a country had lots of forests, for example, it should make things from wood and import goods made from materials it lacked.

The idea of free trade suggested that, if the global economy grew, the benefit would be shared out among all countries. Some might benefit more than others from particular forms of trade, but in the end they would all be better off. This belief has dominated economics for more than 200 years—although virtually all countries continued to use some forms of protectionism to protect key parts of their economy, such as agriculture.

The Scottish economist Adam Smith began the idea of a free market, with no outside regulations.

TRADE WARS

A World Crash?

President Trump was not the first modern leader to want to protect his country's economy. However, the US economy is so large that his decision to impose tariffs on China alarmed many economists. They believe there is a danger that the effects of any trade war will rapidly spread. The Chinese, for example, reacted to US tariffs by placing their own tariffs on US imports to China. This might eventually lead to a slowdown in trade around the world, as other countries also put up barriers to trade.

This has happened before. In the late 1920s, the US economy suddenly slowed after a boom, or a long period of growth. In 1930, the United States introduced tariffs on imports to try to keep sales of US goods high. Instead, the act had the effect of damaging other economies, which could no longer sell their goods in the United States. Instead of helping the US economy perform better, the move had the effect of spreading the economic slow-down around the world. The Great Depression had begun. It lasted for more than a decade.

Unemployed men stand in line for free food during the Great Depression. At its peak, one-quarter of US workers were out of work.

TRADE WARS

✓ DEFENDING THE STEEL INDUSTRY

In March 2018, Donald Trump called for protectionist measures to protect the US steel industry. He argued that industries such as steel are so important to the United States that they should not be threatened by free trade. Trump tweeted: "We must protect our country and our workers. Our steel industry is in bad shape. IF YOU DON'T HAVE STEEL, YOU DON'T HAVE A COUNTRY!"

✗ THE STEEL INDUSTRY IS NOT THE PRIORITY

In May 2018, Donald J. Boudreaux and Nita Ghei of George Mason University defended free trade. They wrote in an article entitled *The Benefits of Free Trade* that steel companies had quit the industry because of high fixed costs and competition within the United States. Tariffs on imported steel would only increase costs in steel-using industries, which employ 13 million Americans. Only 140,000 people are employed in the US steel industry.

WHAT'S YOUR VIEWPOINT?

Do you agree with President Trump's viewpoint, or that of the academics? Use the prompts below to help form your viewpoint.

- President Trump claims that not having a steel industry would harm the country. What problems might there be with only importing steel?
- Boudreaux and Ghei say steel tariffs harm more people than they protect. Should the minority be protected at the expense of the majority?
- If the problem with the steel industry is not free trade but fixed costs and competition, as the academics say, what can be done about it?

The theory behind free trade is that it benefits everyone, not just one side or the other.

TRADE WARS

CHAPTER TWO
FREE TRADE

For more than 200 years, most countries have supported the idea of free trade. In its most basic form, free trade does not place any limits on imports or exports. It is based on Adam Smith's idea that the market should be free.

Smith argued that trade should not be regulated by government. He said prices would be set by the level of demand for a particular good. If enough people wanted to buy something, its price would rise. If goods were too expensive, however, they would not sell. If they were too cheap, the manufacturers would not be able to afford to stay in business. Smith's approach is now known as classical economics, and Smith as the father of economics.

Containers wait to be loaded onto ships in the port at Shanghai in China.

Lack of Barriers

Free trade is based on the idea that there should be no barriers to buying and selling goods between countries. The most common barriers to trade include tariffs and quotas on imports. However, not all barriers to free trade are measures taken directly against imports. Others are created in other ways, such as by regulations. For example, some countries introduce regulations on goods that favor particular suppliers.

European nations such as the United Kingdom will not accept US meat products treated with particular chemicals, for example. Other countries help domestic firms by giving them money to help keep their costs down, so they can sell their goods more cheaply. These payments are called subsidies.

Another obstacle to trade comes when a government creates a situation in which a market is controlled by a limited number of businesses. If one company controls a market, it is known as a monopoly. If a group of companies control a market, it is called an oligopoly. For example, in many US cities and districts, the local government has given a monopoly to utility companies to supply services such as power, water, and cable. In this situation, it is almost impossible for a new supplier to join the market, even if can provide a better or cheaper service.

Trade Agreements

One common feature of free trade is the creation of trade agreements. These agreements set up free trade between two or more countries. NAFTA ensures free trade among the United States, Canada, and Mexico, for example. The European Union (EU) brought together 28 member states in a single trading area, although Great Britain was due to exit in 2019, reducing the total to 27. Even in free trade areas, however, many countries use regulations to try to protect certain types of industries.

Regulations often restrict the international movement of foodstuffs such as meat.

TRADE WARS

Free Trade in Action

Trade blocs such as NAFTA and the EU are the height of the idea of free trade. In the EU, for example, laws across Europe ensure that goods, services, and capital, or money, can move freely between all member countries. As part of the arrangement, people are also allowed to move freely to any of the member countries and work there. Nineteen of the member states use the same currency, the euro. This protects them from paying fees to exchange one currency for another.

The EU grew out of arrangements created after World War II (1939–1945) to promote cooperation among former enemies. After the war, the idea of removing barriers appealed to many people. By the early 2000s, however, some European politicians became suspicious of the EU. Politicians in richer states such as Germany, Great Britain, and the Netherlands argued that the wealth of the union was damaged by weaker economies, such as Greece. They also said that immigrants from other parts of the EU were working for low wages, taking jobs from their citizens.

Free trade is often more popular with economists than it is with politicians. Economists believe that free trade will improve wealth for all. Politicians have to face voters who do not believe the theory. They believe that cheap foreign labor or cheap goods from abroad threaten their jobs.

European Union flags fly outside the headquarters of the EU in Brussels, Belgium.

14

FREE TRADE

Belgians protest a free trade agreement between the EU and Canada in 2016.

Negative Views

Free trade is also often criticized by people from poorer economies. They are worried that they have no protection against richer countries exploiting their materials and their workers. For example, Mexican labor unions complain that US employers in Mexico keep wages low to keep costs down for US consumers. Meanwhile, China uses its greater wealth to buy valuable resources such as copper from African countries such as Zambia. Although this brings money to those countries, it prevents them from developing their own industries. In some cases, they can no longer afford to buy their own resources.

WHAT'S THEIR VIEWPOINT?

The Scottish economist Adam Smith published *The Wealth of Nations* in 1776. The book laid the basis for free market economics. Smith believed free trade would allow countries to produce what they could cheaply, and import other goods. He used wine as an example: "Very good grapes can be raised in Scotland, and very good wine too can be made of them at about thirty times the expense for which at least equally good wine can be brought from foreign countries. Would it be a reasonable law to prohibit [ban] the importation of all foreign wines, merely to encourage the making of claret and burgundy [red wines] in Scotland?"

15

TRADE WARS

Protecting Free Trade

The World Trade Organization (WTO) was created in 1995 to replace the General Agreement on Tariffs and Trade (GATT), which was set up in 1947 to promote free trade around the globe. Today, the WTO has 164 member countries. It provides a set of rules for international trade and a means of figuring out disputes between members.

In 2018, US President Donald Trump threatened to withdraw from the WTO. He claimed it was set up "to benefit everybody but us." The president was unhappy that the WTO often ruled against the United States when other countries complained about US restrictions on trade. This was true, but when the United States complained about trade restrictions by other countries, it usually won its case. Trump was particularly concerned the WTO would say his new tariffs on Chinese goods broke the rules.

The EU suggested that the WTO should be reorganized. The Europeans said this would remove the bias that worried President Trump. They argued it was vital to preserve the WTO to protect global free trade.

Protectionist measures such as checks on imports at borders slow down the movement of goods.

FREE TRADE

✓ FREE TRADE CUTS THE COST OF PRODUCTION

Adam Smith believed that there was a basic rule underlying the theory of free trade. This was the relative cost of producing goods in one place or in another. In *The Wealth of Nations*, he wrote: "It is the maxim [rule] of every prudent [wise] master of a family, never to attempt to make at home what it will cost him more to make than to buy ... What is prudence [wisdom] in the conduct of every private family, can scarce [hardly] be folly [foolish] in that of a great kingdom."

✗ FREE TRADE CREATES OTHER PROBLEMS

In August 2018, UK journalist Richard Partington wrote about free trade in *The Guardian*. He highlighted two areas in which importing goods might not be the best way to carry out trade. The first area was national security. He felt it was unwise, for example, for a country to import all the steel that it used for its tanks. The second area was jobs, as each country should make sure it supports jobs for its own citizens.

WHAT'S YOUR VIEWPOINT?

Smith and Partington take opposing views about the benefits of free trade. Consider these points to see which view you most agree with.

- Adam Smith argues that countries should take the same approach to finance as families. Can you think of cases when this might not be true?
- Richard Partington highlights national security. What types of industries do you think are vital for a country to control for its own security?
- Partington also mentions the loss of jobs to foreign workers. Is it justified to make goods that cost more if it helps protect jobs?

Although most countries support the idea of free trade, many also take steps to protect their own industry.

17

TRADE WARS

CHAPTER THREE
CHINA

For years before he became president, Donald Trump criticized China for the way it carried out trade. He said the Chinese government kept labor costs low to steal US jobs. He also said the Chinese government deliberately made it more expensive for the Chinese to buy US imports.

The United States had bought $506 billion of Chinese imports in 2017—the year Trump became president. China, on the other hand, only bought $130 billion of goods from the United States. That created a trade deficit, or loss, of $376 billion. Trump said the Chinese were putting US jobs and businesses at risk by selling goods cheaper than they could be made in the United States.

A Huge Economy

China had already overtaken the United States as the world's largest economy. Its population of 1.4 billion people provided both a source of cheap labor and a huge market for Chinese goods.

In 2011, China became the world's largest producer of steel. Chinese steel made up 45 percent of the global total.

Americans and people in other countries were eager to buy cheap Chinese products such as computers. This created demand for Chinese imports. To observers such as Donald Trump, this demand seemed artificially created. The Chinese government cut the price of exports by deliberately keeping the value of the Chinese currency, the yuan, low.

At the same time, many Western firms want to do business in China because of its combination of low costs and a huge market. The Chinese often insist that Western firms become partners with Chinese firms. Western firms have to share their technology and designs with their Chinese partners. In this way, in Trump's words, the Chinese "steal" Western technology.

The growth in the Chinese economy has created a booming middle class in cities such as Beijing.

Suspicion of China

Many countries are suspicious of China's aims. From 1949 until 1978, China was a communist country in which the state controlled all business, agriculture, and trade. The result was often disastrous. Many Chinese were poor and hungry. In 1978, China began to encourage privately owned business. The Chinese economy grew quickly in the 1980s and 1990s. By the 2000s, it was growing quicker than any other economy in the world. Its growth also helped that of its neighbors in East Asia. For many people in the United States and Europe, this was a sign that a new global superpower had been born. The Chinese specialized in heavy industry and manufacturing. They produced many goods that they could sell around the world. Meanwhile, within China, a new class of comparatively wealthy workers appeared.

TRADE WARS

China and the US Economy

Many people worry that China's economic expansion will harm the rest of the world. China is becoming involved in other countries' economies. For example, China has bought metals from around the world to help the rapid growth of its cities. The Chinese have even built railroads in African countries to move metals from mines to ports. Some people say China treats other countries in the same way that Western countries used to treat their colonies, as a supply of cheap resources.

One of China's specialties is electronics, which it makes more cheaply than Western factories can.

However, China's international trade is even more complicated. Countries trade their currencies in much the same way as other goods. China has bought so many dollars that it is one of the major sources of income for the US Treasury. China owns $1.8 trillion, which gives it considerable influence over the US economy. If China stopped buying dollars or sold the dollars it has, the value of the dollar would fall. Banks in the United States might raise interest rates, which set the cost of borrowing money. Making it more expensive to borrow dollars would help protect the value of the currency. However, many companies borrow money to pay for materials before their goods can be sold. If the cost of borrowing rose, they might lose money or even go out of business. That might start a recession in which US customers would stop buying both US and Chinese goods.

China wants to avoid a recession, so it keeps buying dollars—and helping support the US economy. It is not unusual for countries to be linked to one another in this way, but the sheer size of China's influence worries some US economists.

Stealing Jobs

Many Americans are unhappy at China's role in the US economy. China has now replaced the United States as the world's leading economy. After the end of World War II, the United States was the world's major superpower and greatest manufacturing power. However, between 1998 and 2010, the number of people employed by US manufacturing fell by 34 percent. Many of these jobs were outsourced, or sent to places such as India and China, where costs are lower.

Many people agree with President Trump that China threatens the economic status of the United States. One report estimated that sending jobs overseas together with cheap Chinese imports cost the US economy 2.4 million jobs between 1999 and 2011. However, this was only a part of the total of about 6 million manufacturing jobs lost in the United States over the same period.

A Chinese worker assembles car engines.

WHAT'S THEIR VIEWPOINT?

Even before he became US president in 2017, Donald Trump was very critical of how China carried out international trade. He was particularly concerned that China sold far more to the United States than it bought from the United States. In his book *Crippled America* (2015), Trump spelled out his objections. In his opinion, China had destroyed US industries by manufacturing the same goods more cheaply, made possible by the fact that labor is much cheaper in China than the United States. By doing so, he argued, China had cost tens of thousands of Americans their jobs.

TRADE WARS

Tariffs for China

In March 2018, President Trump ordered a 25 percent tariff to be placed on steel imports and 10 percent on aluminum. The tariffs were mainly aimed at China. Trump hoped that making imported metals more expensive would force US companies to buy US steel and encourage the industry. However, it would also make metals more expensive for US manufacturers, driving up prices of goods made in the United States.

China imposed tariffs of its own on US agricultural goods, such as soybeans, pork, and cotton. It also placed tariffs on airplanes and automobiles. This will make it more expensive for US companies to sell goods in China.

Economists worried that tariffs might spark a trade war. If the Chinese decided to put tariffs on technology firms such as Apple, for example, there could be huge effects. If Apple's income fell in China, it might have to raise prices in the rest of the world to make up its losses. That might lead to economic disruption in more countries.

China is the biggest market in the world for tech products such as the iPhone.

✓ CHINA CHEATS AT WORLD TRADE

In June 2017, China expert Steven W. Mosher told *Fox News* that the Chinese government "cheats" at industry by giving cheap loans and energy to Chinese factories. It also, he claimed, let its factories ignore environmental, health, and safety standards. In addition, he argued, China is "stealing" valuable technologies from other countries, making them world leaders in industries from computers to shipbuilding.

✗ CHINA'S ACTIONS ARE JUSTIFIED

James Bacchus is a former chief judge for the WTO. In 2018, he wrote an opinion piece for *Bloomberg News* in which he said that it was completely fair and lawful for China to want to become one of the world's leading economies. In the past, China had been exploited by Western countries. Now those same countries were just feeling threatened by a stronger China.

The Chinese yuan is linked to the value of the US dollar, keeping the two economies closely aligned.

WHAT'S YOUR VIEWPOINT?

Do you agree with Steven W. Mosher or James Bacchus? Use the prompts below to help form your viewpoint.

- Steven W. Mosher calls China a cheat. Do you think such language is a useful way to discuss trade?
- James Bacchus suggests that China's actions may be encouraged by its past treatment. Would a desire to catch up justify China's "cheating"?
- Mosher lists ways in which China cheats at business. If China's government gives businesses cheap energy and low safety standards, should the US government do the same for US companies?

TRADE WARS

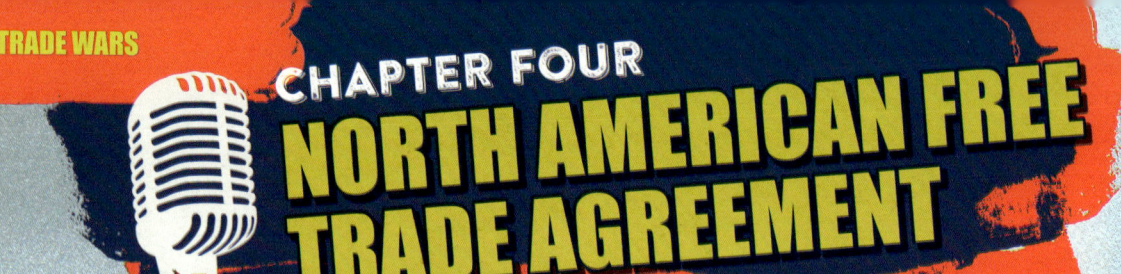

CHAPTER FOUR
NORTH AMERICAN FREE TRADE AGREEMENT

The North American Free Trade Agreement (NAFTA) was created to encourage easy trade among the United States and its neighbors, Mexico and Canada. The United States has by far the largest economy of the three. Canada is rich in resources, particularly wood and wood products, agricultural produce, and minerals. Mexico is the poorest of the three countries, and is classed as an emerging market. It has cheap labor to work in factories. When the deal was signed in 1993, it was the largest free trade agreement in the world.

Under the terms of the agreement, the three countries dropped all tariffs on goods that originated within a member country. This was a dramatic change. At the time, Mexico charged more than 250 times more tariffs on US imports than the US charged on goods from Mexico. The deal also agreed that companies in any of the three countries could bid for work in all three, and agreed to give the same treatment to investors from the other countries as to investors from their own country. NAFTA made it easier for business travelers to move around between the three countries, but it also contained laws to protect copyright, which is the right of a company or individual to control the sales of an invention or idea.

Twenty years after NAFTA was signed, 95 percent of economists said it had helped most Americans.

NORTH AMERICAN FREE TRADE AGREEMENT

An American Idea

The original idea for NAFTA came from the United States, where it was suggested in 1984 by then-president Ronald Reagan. Part of the thinking behind NAFTA was that it would benefit all three countries. It would reduce trading costs and increase investment in businesses. That would help make the whole of North America more competitive in the global marketplace.

One reason Reagan believed it would benefit the United States to create a free-trade area with its neighbors was the possible economic threat created by the rise of other powerful trading countries. In particular, he was alarmed by the growth of the European Economic Community (EEC), a free-trade association originally dominated by France and Germany. In 1993, the EEC became the EU. Membership brought European nations many economic advantages, such as free trade and free movement of labor.

Ronald Reagan believed NAFTA was necessary for the US economy to be competitive.

By 2007, the EU had grown to include 28 member countries. In that same year, it replaced the United States as the world's largest economy. In 2015, the top place passed to China. Supporters of NAFTA claim that it helped the North American economies compete with these two powerful economies, as well as with other developing economies in countries around the Pacific or in South Asia. Without the boost given by NAFTA, some economists argue, the United States would have been left behind by the emerging economic powers.

TRADE WARS

A New NAFTA

In August 2018, the United States said it had renegotiated NAFTA with Mexico. In September, Canada joined the new agreement. This was the United States–Mexico–Canada Agreement (USMCA). President Trump called the deal "historic." He said "[It] will bring all three Great Nations into competition with the rest of the world." Trump claimed the threat of tariffs had forced Mexico and Canada to replace NAFTA.

USMCA made it easier for US farmers to sell their dairy products in Canada.

Some economists argued that the new deal was almost the same as NAFTA. However, there were key changes. In car making, more than 75 percent of a car's parts had to be made in North America. In addition, almost half a car had to be made by workers earning wages of at least $16 an hour. This change aimed to reduce the difference between labor costs in the United States and Mexico. It appealed to US car workers, but it also boosted the Canadian car-parts industry and meant Mexican workers would earn more.

The USMCA also allowed US farmers to sell some dairy products to Canada—though not as much as they wanted. It made it cheaper for people to shop online without paying duties, or import fees. It offered the possibility that the US would lift tariffs on steel and aluminum, and gave added protection to the copyright of US pharmaceutical products in Mexico and Canada.

NORTH AMERICAN FREE TRADE AGREEMENT

USMCA IMPROVES ON NAFTA

Matthew Walther writes for *The Week*. In October 2018, he compared USMCA favorably to NAFTA, saying it benefited mainly the wealthy and the middle classes. He wrote that a very important fact about USMCA is that it actually tries to protect the rights and well-being of all workers, not just the workers of the United States.

 USMCA DOES NOT IMPROVE ON NAFTA

David Fickling writes for Bloomberg.com. He assessed USMCA as being little different from NAFTA—and in keeping with globalization rather than protectionism. He felt that, like other trade agreements made by the Trump administration, while the agreement was said by Trump's team to be "historic" the changes were really only "cosmetic." He felt that globalists, who often disagreed with Trump's opinions on trade, should actually be pleased.

WHAT'S YOUR VIEWPOINT?

Matthew Walther and David Fickling have different views of USMCA. Which do you agree with? Use the prompts below to form your viewpoint.

- Matthew Walther says that USMCA aims to protect all workers. Why should US workers care about workers in Mexico or Canada?
- David Fickling thinks there is a difference between how President Trump describes USMCA and what it says. Why might this please globalists?
- If changes to NAFTA are "cosmetic," did it really need to be changed?

USMCA includes about 490 million people. The population of the EU is about 508 million.

29

TRADE WARS

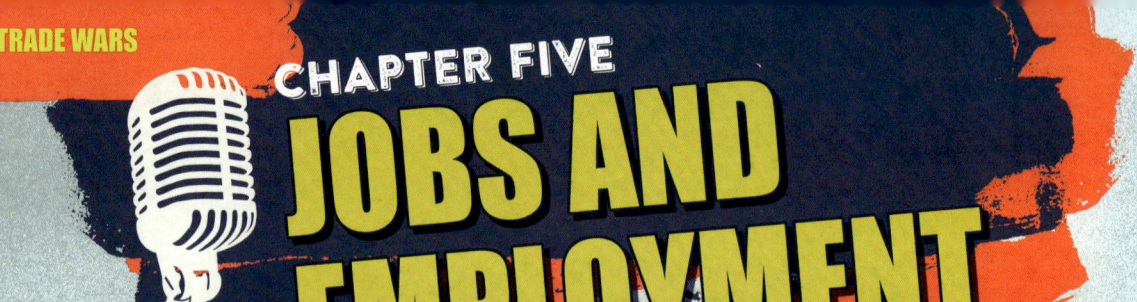

CHAPTER FIVE
JOBS AND EMPLOYMENT

President Donald Trump came to office in January 2017 promising to force US companies to keep their jobs at home. He said they had been sending jobs overseas. In places such as Mexico or East Asia, labor costs are cheaper, so companies can save money. This means US consumers can buy cheaper goods, but it puts US workers out of jobs.

The employment rate is an important measure of economic performance. People with jobs earn money and help raise national production. The more they earn, the more they spend, the more they save, and the more taxes they pay. The more production grows, the larger the economy. On the other hand, unemployed workers have less money and often face difficulties in living rewarding lives.

About 80 percent of US jobs today are in the service sector, which includes hospitality.

Sectors of the Economy

Traditionally, jobs are divided into parts of the economy called sectors. The primary sector is concerned with natural resources, and includes agriculture, mining, and forestry. The secondary sector, heavy industry and manufacturing, includes factories that make anything from cars to TVs, brooms, and furniture.

JOBS AND EMPLOYMENT

The tertiary (third) sector provides services that help meet the needs of people. It includes people who work in stores and restaurants, banks, and financial companies. Public service jobs include people who work for federal or local government, such as teachers, police officers, and National Park rangers.

In the past, many US jobs have been in the primary and secondary sectors. These jobs were often concentrated in areas such as the coalfields of Pennsylvania. From the late 1800s to the late 1900s, these industries were major employers in some communities. In the late 1900s, however, many of these jobs moved overseas, where natural resources were easier to find and labor costs were cheaper.

Disappearing Jobs

Around 1850, more than 66 percent of US workers were in the primary sector. Today, that figure is only 2 percent. Only about 15 percent of Americans now work in the secondary sector. About 80 percent of jobs are in the tertiary, or service, sector. People worry that the United States is becoming too dependent on imported goods and materials. That means more US wealth is going to other countries to buy exports. This increases the trade deficit, which is the difference between how much is imported into the country and how much is exported. However, economists say it is usual for the number of people working in the primary and secondary sectors to fall as a country's economy develops.

Abandoned mines and factories became common sights in the Midwest and Northeast United States.

TRADE WARS

Moving Jobs Overseas

Since the 1980s, about 14 million US jobs have been outsourced. Some are manufacturing jobs. Others include computer support departments and call centers, which are often set up in countries such as India, which have large numbers of trained, English-speaking staff.

Critics of outsourcing complain that it damages both economies. It removes jobs from US workers, but creates a risk that workers in other countries are exploited, or taken advantage of. Workers overseas are sometimes made to work in what are called "sweatshops." These are factories in which unskilled workers, including children, are forced to make goods such as jeans and sneakers for tiny amounts of money. They have little health and safety protection and no labor unions to protect their rights.

Taking a Stand

Donald Trump came to the White House determined to keep US jobs from being sent abroad. He promised to revive dying industries such as coal mining and iron making in the so-called Rust Belt of the Midwest and the Northeast. President Trump criticized

A US worker makes truck parts in a factory in Indiana. Such jobs are in decline in the United States.

32

JOBS AND EMPLOYMENT

WHAT'S THEIR VIEWPOINT?

Gary Pisano is a professor at Harvard Business School. In 2011, he gave an interview to the school magazine about the effect of outsourcing jobs to other countries. For any individual company, he said, it often costs less to outsource production to a foreign supplier, as costs are usually lower overseas. However, if every company does that, there is a loss of jobs in the United States and long-term damage to the economy. This may not matter to companies, as they are still making good profits and passing those profits on to their shareholders.

individual companies such as Harley-Davidson for sending jobs abroad. He managed to get other companies to promise to keep more jobs inside the country.

However, it was not clear that the president could force US companies to keep jobs inside the country. The law does not give the government the authority to interfere in the workings of private businesses. US companies say they have a responsibility to their investors—the people who have put their money into the business—to make the most profits. Companies make decisions based on economics, not on politics. If it is cheaper to make goods overseas, they say, that is what they should do. Large US companies say they are part of a global economy, in which resources, manufacturing, and sales can happen anywhere in the world.

When Harley-Davidson moved jobs to Europe, President Trump told Americans to stop buying the company's motorcycles.

33

TRADE WARS

Rise of the Machine

Some economists say the US services sector is thriving, with nearly 90 million jobs. According to classical economic theory, it is better to leave industry and manufacturing to countries that can do it cheaper. They say that the United States should concentrate on service jobs it can do profitably.

Another viewpoint is that the idea that losing jobs to other countries misses the point. The main threat to jobs is not outsourcing but automation and artificial intelligence (AI). Car building and other industrial tasks are already being carried out by robots, and cows can be fed by robot farmhands.

Robots have replaced workers in many plants. Robots do not get tired or bored—and they do not need to be paid.

Work and Leisure

AI is teaching computers to recognize problems and solve them without human help. This may enable machines to do jobs in law and medicine that involve studying records and diagnosing problems. Employment experts suggest it is inevitable that machines will replace human workers in the future, from driverless trucks to robot housekeepers in hotels and clerks in offices. Some people worry about the results for the employment market, but others are more positive. They see a future in which everyone has more leisure time to enjoy themselves.

JOBS AND EMPLOYMENT

✓ OUTSOURCING IS THE GREATEST THREAT

Businessman Michael Lewis discussed outsourcing on the Money Crashers website. He wrote that if we do not protect manufacturing jobs from offshoring (sending jobs abroad), we will go on to lose service jobs to offshoring, too. Many Americans employed in services do not think their jobs could be done abroad, but in fact, the reality is that more than 28 million service jobs are at risk.

✗ OUTSOURCING IS NOT THE PROBLEM

Kimberly Amadeo is an expert on the US economy at the *Balance*. In August 2018, she wrote about the decline in US manufacturing jobs. She argued that, although some jobs were lost due to offshoring, many others were lost to computers, robots, and bioengineering. She felt that ending offshoring would not bring back all the "decent" jobs that have been lost and that instead we should train US workers in jobs such as robotics and computing.

This robot acts as a security guard on a Samsung property in Silicon Valley, California.

WHAT'S YOUR VIEWPOINT?

Michael Lewis is a businessman, while Kimberly Amadeo studies social change. Who do you think has the most convincing viewpoint?

- Michael Lewis says the loss of manufacturing jobs will lead to the loss of service jobs. Why might he think this will inevitably happen?
- Kimberly Amadeo lists a number of reasons for the loss of jobs. Do you think retraining US workers for new types of jobs is a good idea?
- Amadeo makes the point that it is important to bring back "decent" jobs rather than just any jobs. What do you think makes a job "decent"?

35

TRADE WARS

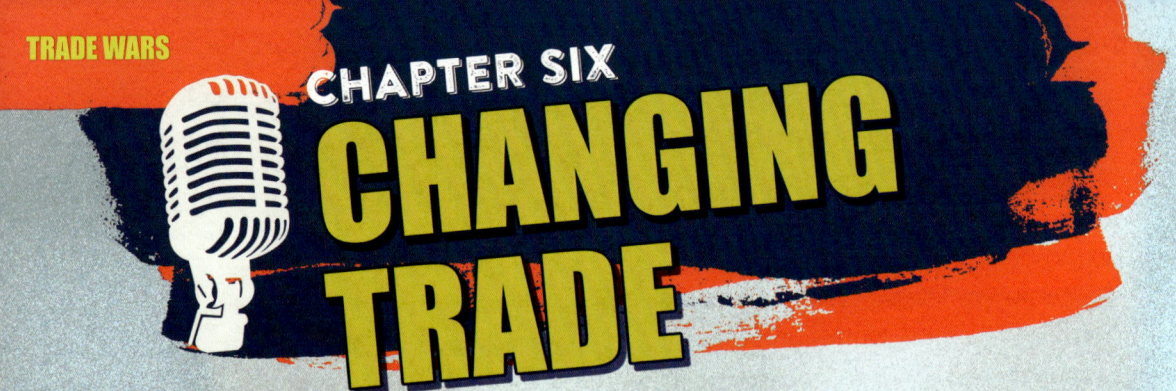

CHAPTER SIX
CHANGING TRADE

Donald Trump began his presidency at the start of 2017 determined to change the way the United States traded with other countries. He wanted to use tariffs and regulations to protect jobs for US workers. He wanted to buy fewer goods from China, and to change the terms of NAFTA. Restoring the United States to a leading position in the world economy was part of a wider campaign called "Make America Great Again."

Many voters shared the president's concerns. However, some experts said Trump's views about the US economy were out of date. They said he was fighting the wrong battle. The whole world economy was changing, and the United States needed to be ready to take advantage of any opportunities it might bring. According to these critics, Trump should stop thinking about the US national economy and think about the whole global economy.

Demonstrators in New York City in 2011 protest the greed of banks on Wall Street.

CHANGING TRADE

A Global Economy

In the last several decades, a process known as globalization has taken place. This means trade takes place freely everywhere. The result is to make borders less important. Firms can operate nearly everywhere, no matter where they are based. They find ideas, materials, and labor in the best or cheapest places and sell goods around the world. Some people see this as a positive development that helps global economic growth and provides value for consumers. Others, however, see it as a dangerous situation in which businesses operate beyond the law. If one country tries to regulate a business, it simply moves its operations to another country.

One criticism of the global economy is that chains such as Starbucks look the same all over the world.

Negative Side of Globalization

In 2008, banks crashed around the world. US banks had begun to bundle up bad loans and sell them as packages to other banks. When lenders failed to pay back what they owed, the banks ran out of money. The crash soon spread around the world because the financial markets were international. All banking systems were connected to others. Governments had to step in to support the banks, at huge costs to taxpayers. The crisis gave a glimpse of the dangers of a globalized economy.

In 2011, the Occupy movement began in New York City. The movement protested the ability of banks to avoid legislation that would force them to act more responsibly. Thousands of protestors marched in cities around the world. They set up camps in the world's most important financial districts. However, they failed to have any lasting impact on the global economy.

TRADE WARS

Rise of E-Commerce

The process of globalization was accompanied by the rise of the Internet and electronic commerce or e-commerce. By about 2020, global e-commerce sales are expected to reach more than $3.5 trillion. US companies such as Amazon and eBay were among the top 10 e-commerce companies in the world. However, three of the top five companies were based in China: Taobao, Alibaba, and Alipay. More than half of all e-commerce took place in China and the United States, but the value of China's e-trade is more than 1.5 times that of the United States.

Amazon has major facilities all over the world, including this warehouse in Germany.

E-commerce changed international trade, particularly in retail. The Internet offered people a wider range of goods than stores did, and allowed them to compare prices from many sellers and get the best price. It also allowed them to have purchases delivered to their doors. For example, many British customers ordered products from Amazon.com, the US part of Amazon. They figured out the relative values of the UK pound and the US dollar made the purchase cheaper. Within Europe, meanwhile, e-commerce companies chose to locate in countries such as Ireland, which offered tax breaks, or reduced tax bills, and cheap postal costs.

CHANGING TRADE

That changed how firms operated. In the past, for example, a book might be published in the United States months before it appeared in Europe. Now, it is available at the same time everywhere. In some ways, this means businesses have less control over the market.

Negative Effects

Some people worried such developments encouraged piracy, which is when people copy goods and sell them without giving the creators money. Other people worried about the impact e-commerce would have on retail districts and malls. If stores closed, fewer shoppers would visit, and coffee shops and restaurants might also lose business. Eventually, it might become too expensive to run traditional businesses at all. Another worry was that, if companies are creating goods for an international market, goods might lose their individual character, so everything becomes more similar.

WHAT'S THEIR VIEWPOINT?

In 2012, Dr. Madsen Pirie of the Adam Smith Institute, which promotes free trade, made a case that the benefits of globalization go beyond trade itself. He wrote that, when countries form trade links with each other, they also cooperate in other ways, making sure they settle arguments with words rather than weapons. He quoted the 19th century French economist Frédéric Bastiat: "Where goods do not cross frontiers, armies will."

The rise of online shopping has led to changes throughout the whole retail sector.

39

TRADE WARS

A New Economy

Some experts predict that globalization will make trade wars unnecessary because companies will operate on an international scale. Regulations imposed by one country or another will have little effect. In this vision of the future, consumers will benefit by having more choice about what to buy.

Globalization and new technology are only two factors changing the nature of trade. Some observers believe old barriers to trade, such as the cost of starting a business, are changing. This allows new types of businesses to develop. These businesses are often small-scale or run from home. People are using the Internet to start their own businesses, so they work for themselves.

This is creating what is called the "gig economy." In the past, people often worked the same jobs for life. In the future, experts suggest that people will work a range of jobs. They may work for themselves. The rise of the ride-sharing company Uber, for example, has created more than 2 million jobs around the world. These are not traditional jobs, with guaranteed hours and pay, and benefits. They are part of the new economic world.

Uber is convenient for users—but does it provide its drivers with a "real" job?

CHANGING TRADE

✓ THE RISK OF TRADE WARS IS FALLING

In July 2018, *InvestorPlace* reassured investors that global companies such as Coca-Cola would not be damaged by a trade war. *InvestorPlace* stated that, wherever Coca-Cola sells its products, it also makes its drinks and packages them in that country. This means that, even if the cost of aluminum cans goes up in the United States, the effects of a trade war would be very small because only a small portion of the company's profits are from the United States.

✗ ANY TRADE WAR MAY BE SERIOUS

In the UK in July 2018, the *Financial Times* newspaper commented that the danger of a trade war is that protectionist measures will spread. If the United States blocks imports from China, China will sell those goods to other countries, which may then copy the United States in taking protectionist measures. If US tariffs on imported aluminum raise the costs of making cans in the United States, then buyers of aluminum cans may demand protection, too.

WHAT'S YOUR VIEWPOINT?

Both *InvestorPlace* and the *Financial Times* believe a trade war may come. What viewpoint do you most agree with?

- *InvestorPlace* says large companies such as Coca-Cola can survive a trade war. However, should we be more worried about smaller companies?
- The *Financial Times* says the costs of tariffs are passed on to the end users of products. Is it right for end users to ask for protection from price increases?
- If countries other than the United States put up barriers to Chinese imports, what effect might that have on world trade?

The Internet brings together producers and consumers from around the world.

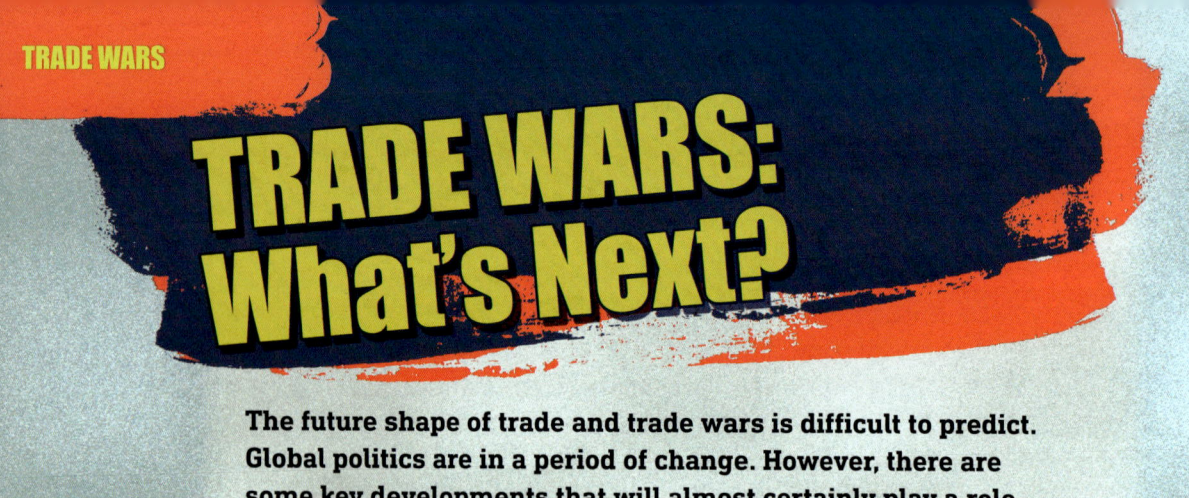

TRADE WARS

TRADE WARS: What's Next?

The future shape of trade and trade wars is difficult to predict. Global politics are in a period of change. However, there are some key developments that will almost certainly play a role.

1 FREE TRADE

Polls suggest that about one-half of Americans are in favor of more free trade rather than the introduction of protectionist measures such as tariffs. However, the United States imposed tariffs on a range of imports in 2017 and 2018. President Donald Trump said they were necessary to protect US jobs. He was also eager for the United States to sell more exports and buy fewer imports. This would reduce the US trade deficit. However, the introduction of tariffs by one of the world's biggest economies might cause a series of retaliatory actions by other countries. If that happens, it is possible that a period dominated by global free trade could come to an end.

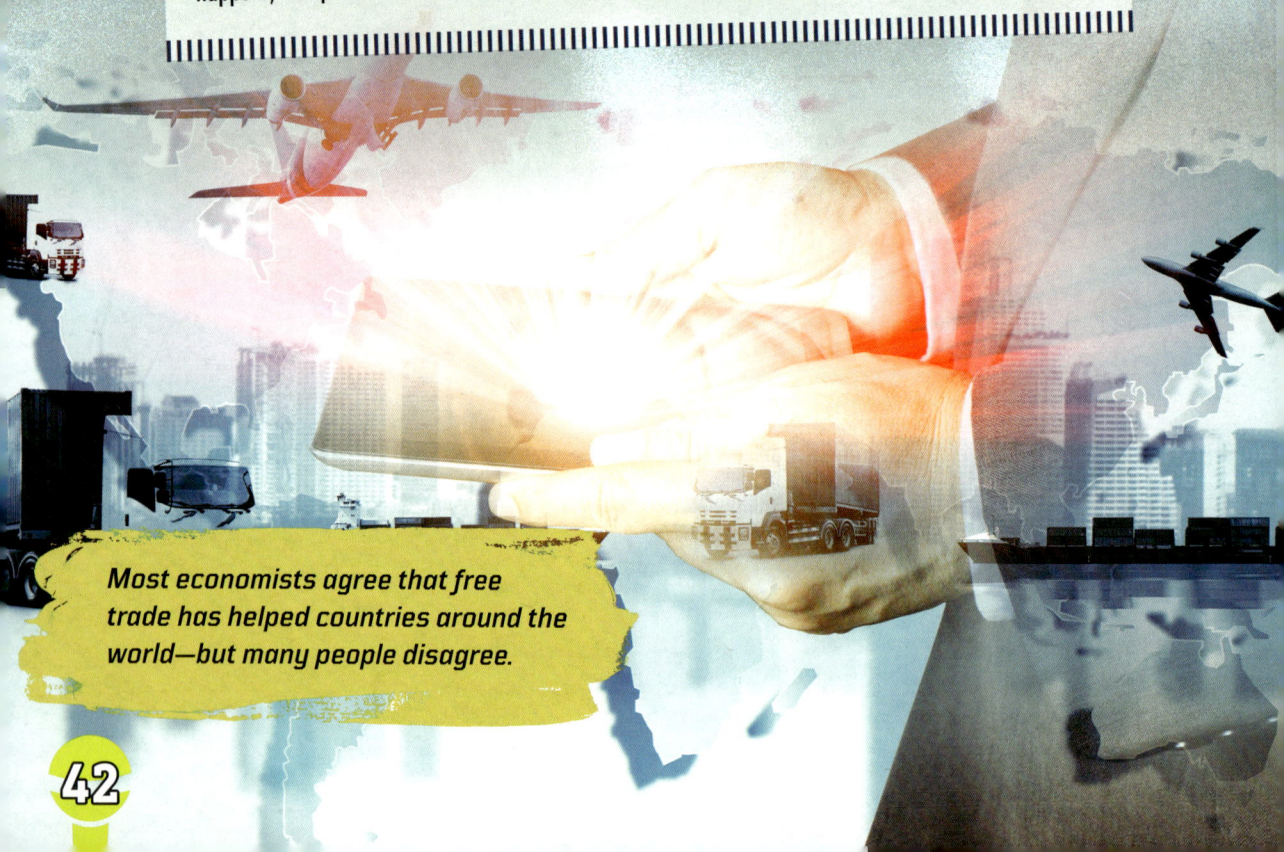

Most economists agree that free trade has helped countries around the world—but many people disagree.

TRADE WARS: WHAT'S NEXT?

2 DEALING WITH CHINA

China's economic power makes it a major concern for other economies. US president Donald Trump has led efforts to force China to obey international rules. He wants the Chinese government to stop subsidizing businesses and to make it difficult for Chinese companies to take technological information from US companies, which he claims they do. Trump imposed tariffs on Chinese imports, but experts suggest those tariffs will lead to US consumers paying higher prices for goods. No one yet knows how Americans will react. Meanwhile, the tariffs China imposed on US goods will also hit sectors of the US economy that export to China, such as agriculture.

3 WORLD TRADE ORGANIZATION

The WTO is a frequent target of Donald Trump's criticism. He claims the organization, which was set up to promote global free trade, acts against US interests. His threat to pull out of the WTO would seriously weaken the organization. Instead, the EU suggested that the WTO should be reformed. It held the first discussions about change in fall 2018. Europe and various countries did not invite the United States or China to the talks.

4 FREE TRADE AREAS

President Trump claimed the creation of the USMCA solved the problems he had identified with NAFTA. Many people disagreed, saying the new deal was not much different than the old one. Elsewhere, meanwhile, free trade was coming under attack. In 2016, the United Kingdom voted to leave the EU and set up its own trade agreements. Politicians in other EU countries also suggested leaving so they could introduce more protectionist policies. Nationalist politicians in many countries echoed Trump's threats to quit the WTO, which the EU was forced to say should be changed.

TRADE WARS

The Future: What's Your Viewpoint?

Some observers are pessimistic about the future of trade wars. Others are more optimistic. These expert viewpoints all predict possible future developments linked to subjects in this book. After reading this book, who do you think is right?

WHAT'S THEIR VIEWPOINT?

Matthew Bey works for a Texas firm that monitors international affairs. In July 2018, he wrote a report on US trade with the EU. He noted that Europe was keen to prevent a trade war between themselves and the United States. Yet, Bey believed, Trump was not concerned with breaking down worldwide trade barriers but only in protecting US industries and markets. His aim was to protect the United States behind tariffs on imported aluminum, steel, and appliances.

WHAT'S THEIR VIEWPOINT?

David Dollar is a China expert at the Brookings Institution. In July 2018, an article Dollar wrote in *The Hill* was featured on the institution's website. It talked about the effect of US tariffs on Chinese imports. Dollar felt that China would easily be able to survive a trade war with the United States as exports to the United States made up only 3 percent of its economy. Instead, Dollar noted, the effect of any trade war between the United States and China would be felt in countries such as Japan, South Korea, and the United States itself, as products and materials from China were heavily used in industries in those countries.

THE FUTURE: WHAT'S YOUR VIEWPOINT?

WHAT'S THEIR VIEWPOINT?

Uri Dadush is a senior fellow at the OCP Policy Center, a think tank based in Morocco. In May 2017, he wrote a briefing paper about the future of globalization. He said that the fastest-growing economies were now developing nations. Their economic growth was driven by a desire to catch up on technological advances and by a young population.

WHAT'S THEIR VIEWPOINT?

E-commerce expert Charles Brewer wrote in January 2018 on the website Future of Ecommerce that the e-market is fully developed in the West and China since about half of US families have Amazon Prime membership and almost half of Chinese people shop online. Brewer believes regions such as South and Southeast Asia and Latin America are where there is still large e-market growth to come.

WHAT'S THEIR VIEWPOINT?

Lucia Widdop works for the organization AI vs Humanity. In June 2018, she wrote about how hard it is to predict how automation will affect the jobs market over the coming years. She sees the biggest challenge as making sure that AI and robots do not take away jobs in many fields. She thinks the answer is likely to be laws that protect human jobs.

WHAT'S YOUR VIEWPOINT?

The future of world trade is complex. The viewpoints on these pages have supporters, but there are also many other viewpoints. Even experts disagree about the impact of tariffs, and how free trade and jobs will look in the future. Use this book as a starting point to carry out your own research in books and online to develop your own viewpoint. Remember, there is no right or wrong answer—as long as you can justify your views.

45

Glossary

administration the government of a particular president
artificial intelligence (AI) the ability of computer systems to perform tasks that usually require a human ability to think
aspirationally showing a desire to achieve success
automation the process of replacing workers with machines
bioengineering using engineering to improve human health
blocs groups of countries acting together
blue-collar workers people who work in industry using their hands
borrowing taking money temporarily
colonies countries that are governed by other countries
communist a supporter of a form of society in which the state owns all businesses
consumers customers who buy goods or services
cosmetic in appearance only
currency the money used in a country
depression a long period of economic decline, or loss
developing economies countries with low living standards but growing trade and industry
domestic taking place inside a country
downstream later in a process
economy a country's business, trade, and finances
emerging market a place where many goods are available for the first time
exploiting using in an unfair way
fixed costs costs that all businesses pay, such as rent
gig economy an economy in which many jobs are short-term
globalists people who believe economies need to work on a worldwide scale
heavy industry the manufacture of large, heavy materials, such as steel
immigrants people who move to settle in a new country
imported brought into a country to be sold
industry the activity of processing raw materials and manufacturing in factories
intellectual property ideas that can be bought and sold
interest rates the cost of borrowing money
interference obstructing
investors people who give money to a business in the hopes of making a profit
labor unions organizations that support workers' rights
legislation laws
loom a frame for weaving textiles
lumber wood that has been cut into lengths
manufactured made in a factory
motives reasons for doing something
nationalist someone who puts their country's needs before any others
national security a country's safety against terrorism, spying, or other attacks
pharmaceutical related to medicines
production the action of making things from raw materials or parts
profits money earned against the cost to make something
recession a period of economic decline
regulated controlled by rules
resources useful materials that occur naturally, such as water or coal
retail selling goods to customers
retaliatory getting back at someone
revenue money raised as income
rhetoric powerful speech
robotics the development of machines to perform tasks
services businesses that take care of customers, such as hotels or restaurants
shareholders the people who own shares of a company
specialize to concentrate on something specific rather than many things
subsidies payments made by governments to help businesses
taxes payments charged by a government
theory an explanation of something
think tank a place where researchers come up with new ideas about a subject
trade the buying and selling of goods
trade deficit the difference between what a country earns from exports and what it spends on imports

For More Information

BOOKS

Cooke, Tim. *Money and Trade* (What's the Big Idea?). New York, NY: Cavendish Square, 2017.

Idzikowski, Lisa. *Globalization and Free Trade* (Introducing Issues with Opposing Viewpoints). New York, NY: Greenhaven Publishing, 2018.

McCoy, Erin L. *Financial Meltdowns* (Top Six Threats to Civilization). New York, NY: Cavendish Square, 2019.

Perritano, John. *Trade, Economic Life, and Globalization* (The Making of the Modern World: 1945 to the Present). Broomall, PA: Mason Crest, 2016.

WEBSITES

China *www.china-family-adventure.com/economy-china.html*
A page about the Chinese economy and how it has become so powerful.

Free Trade *www.bbc.co.uk/news/business-38209407*
The ideas behind free trade and why economists are worried about protectionism.

NAFTA *www.american-historama.org/1990-present-modern-era/nafta.htm*
A collection of fascinating facts about the North American Free Trade Agreement.

Trade Wars *money.howstuffworks.com/who-wins-loses-in-trade-war.htm*
A page about the positive and negative effects of trade wars.

Publisher's note to educators and parents: Our editors have carefully reviewed these websites to ensure that they are suitable for students. Many websites change frequently, however, and we cannot guarantee that a site's future contents will continue to meet our high standards of quality and educational value. Be advised that students should be closely supervised whenever they access the Internet.

Index

African countries 15, 20
agriculture 9, 19, 27, 30, 43
Amazon 38, 45
Apple 22
artificial intelligence (AI) 34, 35, 45
automation 34, 35, 45

barriers, trade 4, 5, 10, 12, 14, 40, 41, 44

Canada 6, 13, 15, 24, 26, 27, 28, 29
cars and car parts 21, 26–27, 28, 30, 32, 34
China 4, 6, 7, 8, 10, 12, 15, 18–23, 25, 33, 36, 38, 41, 43, 44, 45
coal mining 31, 32
copyright 24, 28

depression 5, 10

East Asia 8, 19, 30
eBay 38
e-commerce 38–39, 45
Europe 8, 14, 19, 23, 25, 33, 38, 39
European Economic Community (EEC) 25
European Union (EU) 13, 14, 15, 16, 25, 29, 43, 44
exports 9, 12, 19, 27, 31, 42, 43, 44

forestry industry 27, 30
free trade 4, 5, 6, 9, 11, 12–17, 24–29, 37, 39, 42, 43

gig economy 40
global economy 5, 9, 33, 36–37
globalization 37, 38, 40

Great Britain 8, 13, 14, 41
Great Depression 10

Harley-Davidson 33
heavy industry 19, 30
hospitality industry 30

imported goods 4, 6, 7, 9, 17, 18, 19, 22, 31, 41, 44
international trade 4, 6, 7, 16, 20, 21, 38
iron making 32

jobs 4, 6, 7, 14, 17, 18, 21, 26, 27, 30–31, 40, 45

labor, cheap 5, 14, 18, 24, 26, 27
Lincoln, Abraham 9
lumber 6, 27

manufacturing 19, 21, 23, 26, 30, 32, 33, 34, 35
maquiladoras 27
Mexico 6, 7, 13, 24, 26–27, 28, 29
mining 20, 30, 31, 32

Netherlands 8, 14
North American Free Trade Agreement (NAFTA) 6, 13, 14, 24–29

Occupy movement 36, 37
online shopping 38–39, 45
outsourcing 21, 32–33, 34–35

primary sector 30, 31
protectionism 8–9, 11, 16, 41, 42

quotas 4, 12

Reagan, Ronald 25
recession 20, 21
resources 15, 20, 24, 30
robotics 34, 35

secondary sector 30, 31
service sector 30, 31, 34–35
Silk Road 8
Smith, Adam 9, 15, 17
specializing 8, 19
stealing ideas and technology 5, 8, 19, 21, 23
steel industry 5, 11, 17, 18, 22, 28, 41
subsidies 13, 23, 27

tariffs 4, 7, 10, 11, 12, 16, 22, 24, 27, 41, 42, 43, 44
trade deficit 18, 31, 42
Trans-Pacific Partnership (TPP) 6
Trump, President Donald 6–7, 10, 11, 16, 18, 19, 21, 26, 28, 29, 32–33, 36, 42, 43, 44

Uber 40
United Kingdom 13, 43
United States–Mexico–Canada Agreement (USMCA) 28–29, 43
US Treasury 20

wages 14, 15, 21, 27, 28
Washington, George 9
Wealth of Nations, The 15, 17
World Trade Organization (WTO) 16, 43
World War II 14, 21

yuan 19, 23